SOLUTIONS FOR AMERICA

Handbook

Part I
Social Security

Colonel Michael Mittag

ISBN: 978-1-967349-91-3

Table of Contents

Dedication

This book is dedicated to every American retiree to ensure they retire with dignity and plenty of time to enjoy their remaining days on earth.

Acknowledgment

I want to thank my wife, Shirlyn Mittag, for her continuous encouragement and unwavering support. But, above all, I want to thank God for his mercy, grace, and insight while writing this book.

About the Author

Michael Mittag is a Retired United States Army Colonel with three combat tours to Afghanistan and Iraq. He continues to train our military across the country and overseas.

Michael holds a Master of Science in Agricultural Economics from Texas A&M University. He is an avid reader of philosophy, history, and economics.

Michael's great love of our country drives him to leave it better than when he found it. He is determined to tackle our greatest problems and find real and most suitable solutions for them.

With this book, which is the first in the series of "Solutions for America," he wants to make a real difference by using all his knowledge and passion for the country. He wants to lay down ideas that can become the real deal in terms of solving some of the grave problems Americans are facing now.

Preface

This book is a guide for retired Americans regarding how to increase their social security monthly payments after retirement. This book explains the current model of payments under social security over a normal working American individual's lifetime and what he/she gets after they retire.

The author, a retired United States Army Colonel, presents an innovative idea of eliminating all costs to taxpayers for social security and receiving the payments at least 2 ½ times more in the duration of retirement. To get to these calculations, he considers multiple factors like inflation, interest, and fertility rates. Furthermore, he also reiterates the uniformity in retirement payments for all individuals regardless of their earnings throughout their lifetime, bringing the retirement age to 60 and ensuring the retirement payments are made indefinitely to an individual as long as he/she lives.

The most important factor for this model to remain viable and sustainable is carefully considering the long-term economic downturns and making minor adjustments to ensure those economic pitfalls don't affect the proposed model. It is high time to seriously look at our social security problem and take actionable steps to avoid any bankruptcy due to this fund, as the lives of many American retirees rely on this.

Introduction

What if someone told you that there is a way to increase Social Security monthly payments for retirees by more than 2 ½ times and retire 7 years earlier than usual and cost taxpayers nothing? You would say that this is impossible, but it's not.

In 2023, a single person who made the average wage of $66,100 and retired in 2020 would have paid a total of **$367,000** into Social Security over his or her lifetime.[1]

The average life expectancy of a baby born in the United States in 2022 is 77.5 years. [2]

The average social security payout per month is **$1,976**[3]. The **total average payment received from social security** during 126 months would be 126 x $1,976 per month, which equals **$248,976, provided the individual retires at 67,** which is categorized as **"full retirement."**

Every working individual contributes a total payment of around **$367,000** to US Social Security over their lifetime.

U.S. average total payout received to the individual after retirement for (10.5 years) from social security: **$248,976**

---

[1] https://www.freefacts.org/resources/how-much-money-will-i-pay-into-social-security-and-how-much-will-i-get-out

[2] https://www.cdc.gov/nchs/products/databriefs/db492.htm

[3] https://www.ssa.gov/faqs/en/questions/KA-01903.html

Graph:1

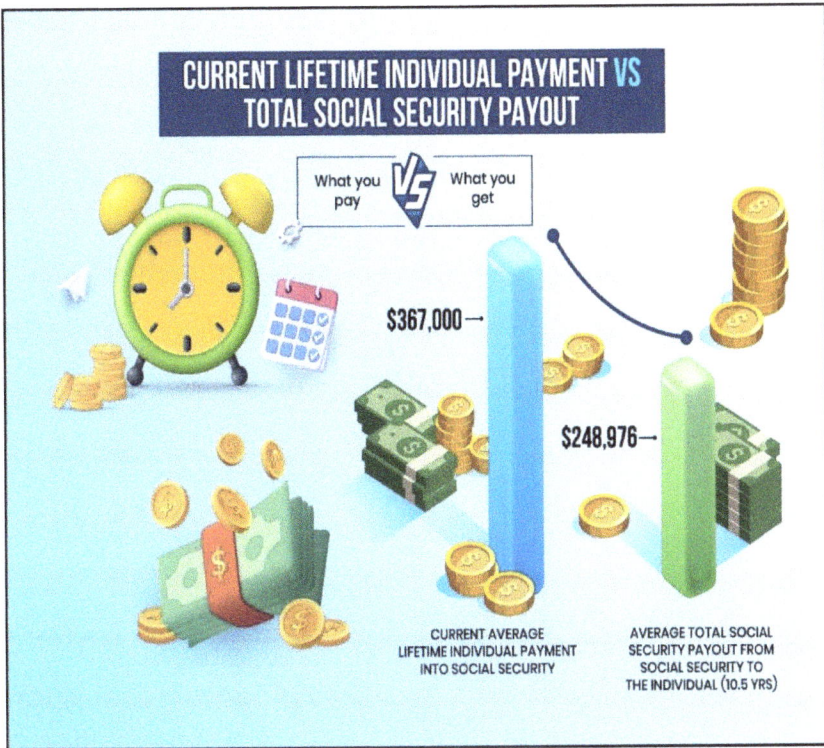

CURRENT LIFETIME INDIVIDUAL PAYMENT VS TOTAL SOCIAL SECURITY PAYOUT

What you pay VS What you get

$367,000

$248,976

CURRENT AVERAGE LIFETIME INDIVIDUAL PAYMENT INTO SOCIAL SECURITY

AVERAGE TOTAL SOCIAL SECURITY PAYOUT FROM SOCIAL SECURITY TO THE INDIVIDUAL (10.5 YRS)

Initial Payment at the Time of Birth

If, on the other hand, every baby born in America was provided with an option of paying one time the amount of **$7,000** at birth instead of paying **$367,000** over their lifetime, the social security account would be worth **$3,422,508.07** at 60 years old with a **10.9%** compounded annual return without any additional payments.

Why 10.9% return? Because from January 1, 1970, to December 31, 2023, the average annual compounded rate of return for the S&P 500®, including reinvestment of dividends, was approximately 10.9%.[4]

Calculation:

☒ Formula: Future Value = Present Value * (1 + Interest Rate) ^ Number of Years

☒ Plugging in values: Future Value = $7,000 * (1 + 0.109) ^ 60

☒ Result: Future Value = $7,000 * (1.109) ^ 60 = $3,422,508.07

---

[4] www.spglobal.com

⁵Graph:2

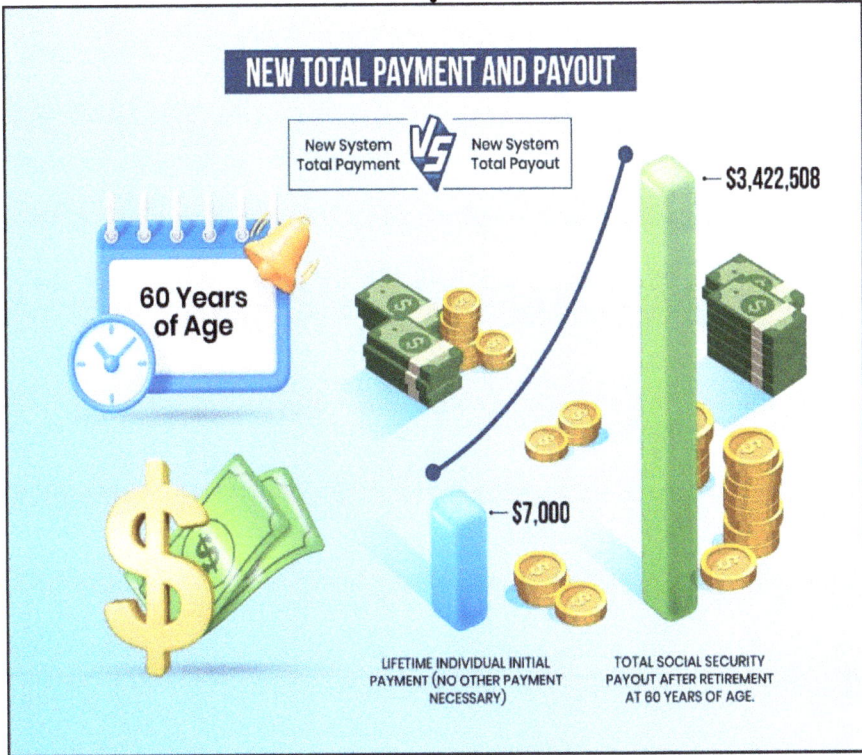

NEW TOTAL PAYMENT AND PAYOUT

New System Total Payment **VS** New System Total Payout

60 Years of Age

$3,422,508

$7,000

LIFETIME INDIVIDUAL INITIAL PAYMENT (NO OTHER PAYMENT NECESSARY)

TOTAL SOCIAL SECURITY PAYOUT AFTER RETIREMENT AT 60 YEARS OF AGE.

---

⁵ https://www.ameriprise.com/financial-news-research/financial-calculators/investment-return-calculator

Real Numbers

But of course, these are nominal numbers, and we must put them into real numbers. We need to make these numbers the same at this moment and 60 years from now. To do that, we need to take inflation into consideration. From 1925 through 2023, the Consumer Price Index (CPI) had a long-term average of 3.0% annually, as the U.S. Bureau of Labor Statistics reported. If we include **3% inflation** with the 10.9% return, our social security account falls from $3,422,508.07 in nominal terms to **$580,912.87** in real terms. But now we can compare a $7,000 initial social security investment for every newborn today with a $7,000 initial social security investment 60 years from now for every newborn.

Graph:3

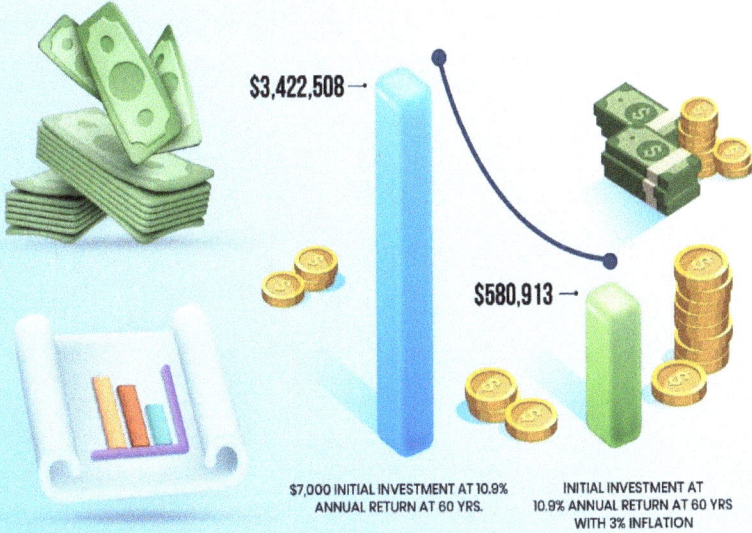

NOMINAL TOTAL PAYOUT VS REAL TOTAL PAYOUT

$3,422,508 →

$580,913 →

$7,000 INITIAL INVESTMENT AT 10.9% ANNUAL RETURN AT 60 YRS.

INITIAL INVESTMENT AT 10.9% ANNUAL RETURN AT 60 YRS WITH 3% INFLATION

Indefinite Payments

If a person retires at 60 years of age, with a social security balance of **$580,912.87** in real terms, and this balance continues to grow at 10.9%, the retiree will have **$63,319.50** to spend each year while keeping the principle the same. This monthly payment of $5,276.63 is more than 2 ½ times the $1,976 average Americans get today in social security. He or she would be able to retire 7 years earlier at 60 rather than the average American today at 67 -"full retirement." Additionally, these payments would go on theoretically indefinitely regardless of how long the retiree lives. It also makes no difference if the individual earned $900 billion over their career or earned no money. Both would get the same **$5,276.63** monthly Social Security retirement check. The retirement check will begin at age 60, regardless of whether the individual continues to work or not. There is no penalty if the retiree continues to work, and the retirement is tax-free.

Graph:4

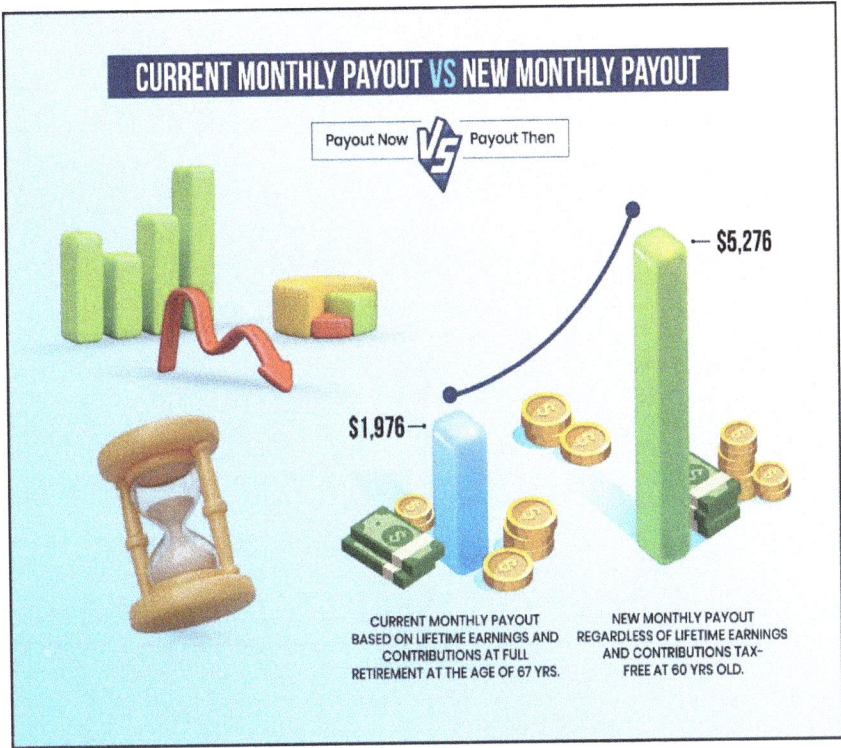

CURRENT MONTHLY PAYOUT VS NEW MONTHLY PAYOUT

Payout Now VS Payout Then

$5,276

$1,976

CURRENT MONTHLY PAYOUT BASED ON LIFETIME EARNINGS AND CONTRIBUTIONS AT FULL RETIREMENT AT THE AGE OF 67 YRS.

NEW MONTHLY PAYOUT REGARDLESS OF LIFETIME EARNINGS AND CONTRIBUTIONS TAX-FREE AT 60 YRS OLD.

Retirees making more than the Average American

The current system penalizes anyone making more than $23,400 [6]per year if they retire "early" before 67 years of age. $5,276.63 per month is **$63,319** per year; it is more than the initial example of the average single American making $66,100 per year because they are paying taxes on their income. The United States Tax Code for 2024 is 22% for any single person earning between $47,151 to $100,525. A single person earning $66,100 would bring home a net after taxes of **$51,558**. The retiree pays no tax on $63,319 per year. Hence, the retiree would be making more than the average single American.

---

[6] https://www.ssa.gov/benefits/retirement/planner/whileworking.html

Graph:5

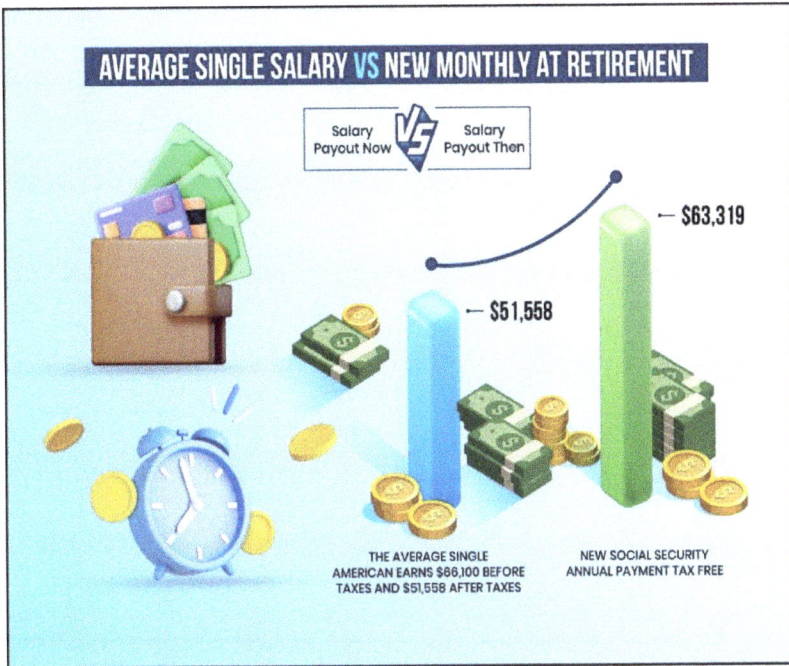

Graph:6

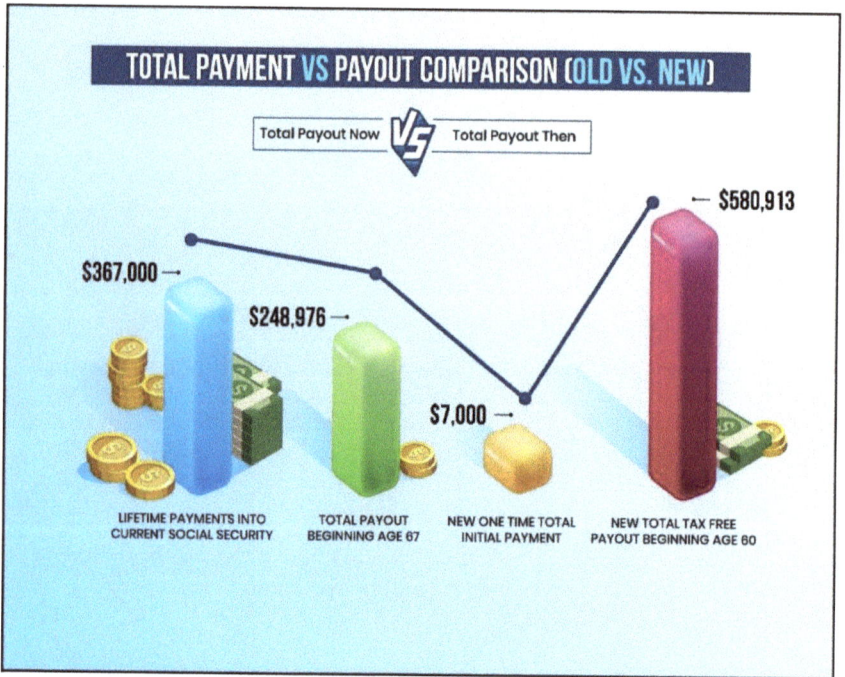

Interest from Index Funds

How do we do it?

There are 3.6 million babies born in the United States every year. This would be a cost of 3.6 million x $7,000 = **$25.2** billion/year. Once the system is fully implemented after 60 years, no payment will be necessary to maintain it. Rather, the interest earned from index funds would be enough to fund social security fully. At the time of death, using the above example, 10% **($58,091.28)** is deducted from each account to fund two newborns in America ($7,000 x 2 = **$14,000**) plus a general fund for families losing a parent **($44,091.28)**. It would account for inflation and ensure that every American newborn gets a fully funded retirement in real terms. The remaining retiree account balance ($580,912.87 - $58,091.28 = **$522,821.59**) is willed to the family upon death.

Graph:7

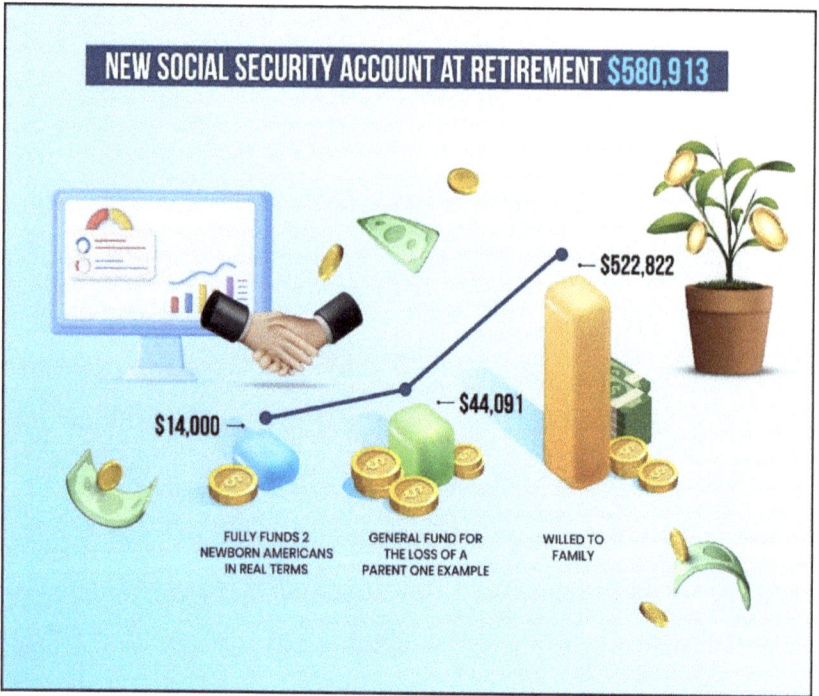

Replacement Rate

To maintain a population, a country needs a total fertility rate (TFR) of about 2.1 children per woman. This is known as the "replacement rate." Our new social security system would allow for a "replacement rate" of 4 since every retiree (male and female) would contribute to 2 newborn babies each back into the system. It allows for substantial population growth, should that ever be the case.

How can we ensure the system remains viable in the long term? One way is adding to the margin of error to account for significant and long-term economic downturns, for example. What happens if we triple each newborn retirement account from $7,000 to $21,000? We would simply deduct 15% instead of 10% from **$580,912.87 and** get **$87,136.93**. This is deducted from each account to fund two newborns in America ($21,000 x 2 = **$42,000**) plus a general fund for families losing a parent **($45,136.93),** for example. This leaves **$493,775.94** to be willed to the family.

Graph:8

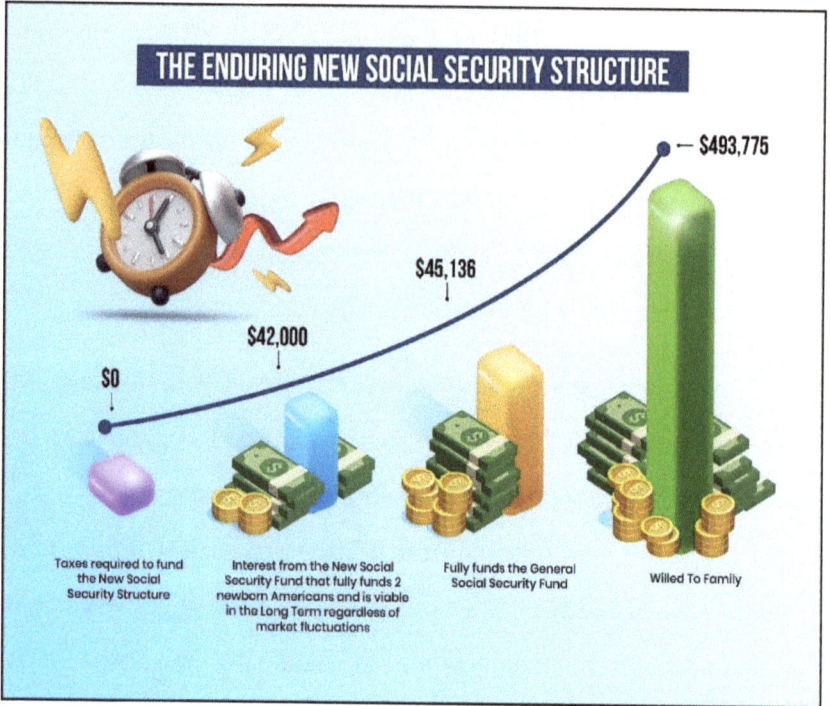

THE ENDURING NEW SOCIAL SECURITY STRUCTURE

$493,775

$45,136

$42,000

$0

Taxes required to fund the New Social Security Structure

Interest from the New Social Security Fund that fully funds 2 newborn Americans and is viable in the Long Term regardless of market fluctuations

Fully funds the General Social Security Fund

Willed To Family

19

Conclusion

Just to add perspective, the $45,136 that every retiree contributes at the time of death to the general fund at 10.9% return with 3% inflation is equal to **$22,408,657.45** in real terms for any family losing a parent or other needs of the general fund. This provides an "escrow account" that fully funds the following:

1. The surviving spouse has an income of the national average ($66,100/year) for the rest of his or her life, regardless of whether the surviving spouse works or not or the spouse remarries, and it shall be tax-free. The surviving spouse will then receive social security at age 60. Other survivors may include children and dependent parents.

2. Each child will have college or trade school paid in full.

3. Disability or blindness.

4. Supplemental Security Income and Medicare.

The principal would then be distributed back into the New Social Security System. Would anyone need life insurance after that?

The $21,000 initial interest payment from the new Social Security Enduring Structure for each American newborn is $10,425,864.20. Even if the stock market went down 94% in the last year before retirement, the retirement in real terms would be more than 2 ½ times our current retirement from Social Security.

20

Moreover, making minor adjustments to the General Fund would cover the costs of Education, Healthcare, Medicare, and Medicaid.

How do we transition to the new social security structure?

1. Tax minerals, oil, natural gas, and other resources from federal lands. The Federal Government currently receives $10 billion per year in revenue. President Trump plans to greatly expand this, and it will likely cover the entire $25.2 billion cost of fully funding social security for every American newborn.

2. Additionally, Use savings from Federal Budget Cuts. Elon Musk is currently proposing $2 trillion in cuts.

3. Furthermore, Congress could pass legislation to fund the new social security structure.

4. Keep the current system in place as a solid transition to the new model. This means that corporations pay 6.2% and individuals pay 6.2%. It would continue for 20 years, at which time workers and corporations could pay progressively less into the system every year until no payments are necessary to fully fund social security. Social security would be fully funded sixty years from now by the compounding interest of the initial $7,000 investment for every newborn.

These are just a few ideas for funding the new social security structure, but there are countless others. If you believe this is a viable option for our current social security problem and wish to act, call your congressman, senator, and even the president. Ask them about their plan and solution for Social Security going bankrupt in just a few more years.

www.ingramcontent.com/pod-product-compliance
Lightning Source LLC
Chambersburg PA
CBHW040759220326
41597CB00029BB/5056